My Night to Cook

Po[barcode] AF450531

Thomas Zimmerman

Acknowledgments

My thanks to the editors of the following publications, where earlier versions of the poems in this book first appeared:

Amphora; *Barren Magazine*; *Beakful*; *Califragile*; *Cape Magazine*; *Changing Light*; *Dadakuku*; *Disturb the Universe*; *8 Poems*; *Eldritch Lake*; *Everything in Aspic*; *Eye Flash Poetry Journal*; *Fish Barrel Review*; *Furtive Dalliance*; *Horror Senryu Journal*; *Hunnybee*; *Inner & Outer Spaces*; *Litmora*; *Lost River*; *The Minison Zine*; *Moonchild Magazine*; *Mystery of Love, History of Hope 2.0*; *Nice Cage*; *Nine Muses Poetry*; *Nocturne: Poetry of the Night*; *Panoply*; *Poetry Sustains*; *Poetry Sustains: Investing in Our Resources*; *The Poetry Village*; *Pulp Poets Press*; *Pulsar Poetry Webzine*; *Pulsebeat Poetry Journal*; *Ragaire Literary Magazine*; *Rasputin: A Poetry Thread*; *Red Wolf Editions*; *Rune Bear*; *Seers and Soothsayers*; *Sum Journal*; *Summer Visions*; *The Unconventional Courier*; *Urtica*; *Wasteland Review*.

Earlier versions of the poems in section III of this book appeared previously in my chapbook *Conjugal Spaces: A Poem* (Zetataurus Press, 2020).

Contents

I.

my night to cook

the bubbling meatball sauce
the sweating bitter ale
the thumping pasta pot's Medusa hair

my night to cook

it's deja vu
ten thousand times
the wheel of fate
it matters little
if i'm coming up or going
down

the morning's blue sky paled to white
and now it's night
i read Li Po all day
the mountain blossoms
mirror rivers
measured sorrow
ladled wine
suffused with beauty
and its mother
death

for now though cooking
is catharsis
i can stir and drink
and play loud music if you're gone

you're gone

the string quartet's called *Intimate Letters*
and this is one to me
or maybe you

after Midtown

i'm thinking of that time in Midtown
i read *Heart of Darkness*
in the hotel bed

next day took photographs
of bricks
a burned out snuggery i loved

then bought three books of poetry
saw works by Rubens Brueghel
Tintoretto Caravaggio

the night before
two members of our favorite band in concert
in a stranger's living room

and how could i forget the morning sex

right now it's late Beethoven
in my earbuds
ale in front of me

the sky inscrutable
from clouds to sun
then bluster
sun again
gods being gods

the music
beauty tempting terror
it's sublime

the boulder and the hill

same copper streaked gray sky
we woke to late

fourth cup of coffee
Haydn in my headphones
football on tv the volume muted
like late autumn hues
like my responses flatlining
to prickings of existence

stubble chinned unshowered and unwise
i'm sagging with the gravity of years

dog licks
wife scolds
dog licks
like Sisyphus we've learned to love
the boulder and the hill
the dash of bitters in the cosmic swill

oh some of this rings false
or doesn't last

the evergreens grow dark
but brighten at the equinox

we're lightly here
but still endure

strong feelings come and go
just breathe

claws

just trimmed your nails this morning
you don't need them
to remember
that we all have claws

reminds you of a conference years ago
a poet told you
there are claws around us
then
how long have you been writing

this before a curt
dismantling of your work
your miniatures lay there
scratched and chipped

the poem the poet liked the best
was one about your death
just sayin'

why not sample it
streams nibble behind my knees

that night the poet read a poem you loved
about kids playing hide and seek

at dusk the parents cry
all in all in

a fine refrain
evading claws
or entering their clutches

cloud music

tempt fate again
unwrap the shadow bands
that bind your high desires

and let your soul ascend
to music in the clouds
to lands invisible to monied eyes
but whole and wholesome
to the searcher seeking light

inspired minds know moaning cellos tell
the groans of Mother Earth
the season's bite that wounds then heals
the water's ebb and swell

both bitter and naive the violin
a door hinge squealing
boy cry thunder rain
downed power lines
a shaken house

and thin the line between
fatigue and breakdown's pain

the god i pray to
told me that she dreams
she's better dead

yet still the star field gleams

dispatch

my dad would have been 95 today
and i'll be 65 next spring

regardless of which Zimmerman's alive
or dead
years fall like rain to swell the river
same mad god still counting drops

now drowned gold sun
dry champagne in your glass
strong ale in mine

i slept in late this morning
haven't showered

mind's a dark pavilion
fairness in the shadows turning blue
and temples gray

i write because i want to feel alive
the poet in the book i'm reading
says the same

new moon late birdsong
whine of tires on the interstate
the bedroom window cracked
to let the night air in

death floating lonely and austere

i feel it pass but know that it and i
will cycle back

this dispatch from the planet
time
my molecules
so slightly all
coheres

eight days no rain

although it's clouding up

you hate to think
that you've been playing sick
with headaches funky stomach

let it pass
be patient
well worn mantras

have you ever tried to strip
the skin from them

venetian blinds hang
cracked as Heaven
giving little light

but Hell's between the ears

your wife is gone
you're left alone to dog sit

on depressive days like these
you try a bit of everything

the streaming string quartet
of course it helps
a cello saws through anything

the dishes in the sink
a mindless blessing
last night's pizza pan still soaking

thoughts aren't real

and if you can't have fun
just get some work done

fallen

today
with sunshot reddened trees
a dog as black as Cerberus asleep
can frame
a vision of the roof of hell we walk

like you
i've fallen through so many times
down to the rafters

madman in the attic
fish boil of the mermaids
in the basement

got my wings singed
cracked my singing
pages written
kindling for my auto da fe

but in the coven
of my mother's house
i thrived in light and shade
i had my father
and my father's name
those myths and maps

in milk in smoke in lamplight
and the daylit mirror
fate and i remade

and still remake me
broken
whole
rebroken
healed

few good things

a sluggish walk in dewy woods with Ann
and Trey
who nearly snagged a fresh dead bird

the sun burned off some brain fog
thoughts began to breach
and then submerged without a word

unshowered stubble chinned
i had a bad night's sleep
Trey licking barking in his dreams.

or maybe it was me
poor poet sad enough
to nurse his ironies and memes

and now black coffee's coursing
through my wan and tepid blood
spring gleam in glacial shade

yet ennui clings like moss
chill hanging on

not hard to see
how few good things get made

how long this search for beauty
truth
gods' signs

ad infinitum

no
just 20 something lines

for now

another Sunday night with beer
and Trey our greyhound

Ann's on Zoom with friends
the pot is thumping with its pasta near al dente
football on tv

a fleeting thought
an image comes
the vibrant yellows reds
and stubborn greens
of trees today
bright sun cool breeze
my hoodie zipped
my morning meds
(two cups of coffee) kicking in

i'm done
with anger and depression
moving past and well above
my baseline suffering

euphoria
yes yes it doesn't last
but in the woods it swallows me

i'm king of space and time
my freed daydreaming mind ascends

the universe
for now
is kind

get lost

the dog and i were walking
in our former neighborhood
about a mile from here
and i got lost of course

but found my mind and got us home

right now
a second beer in front of me
a symphony is streaming
through my kitchen speaker
oven heating for some flatbread pizzas

i'm rereading
my eleventh Seamus Heaney book
just one more left

a friend asks why i read so much
i say to lose
then find
myself

our new red pendant lights
emit a hellfire glow
and i'm a wayward hero
asking questions of the damned

do you ransack your word hoard
are there gems among the rubble

pheasants nesting
in imagination's stubblefield

i bide my time
i'm in a groove
i could explode

there's nothing more
i'd like to do
unless it's more
of this

the great blue whale

the music almost static but i love it

double bass
electric murmurs
like the sounding heart
the breathing trees

the poet that i'm reading says
the other world
is also this one

the great blue whale of the heart
its murmurs squeaks and hums

oh it's all right
if i repeat myself

i sliced heirloom tomatoes earlier today
Dad's big old knife
i sharpened for the job
still glistening like bloodied mercury

so lucky to record this senseless beauty

gray green light
late season's dusk
Atlantic shadows
minor key
dishwasher chugging like a tug
the pregame on tv

Hecate's cat

her black cat
opens its pink mouth and meows
you smell turned earth and Lethean pools

outside
the moon has spilled its silver milk
to rouse
the banshees succubi and ghouls
that hide within
the shadowed woodlands
of your mind

your mother was a witch
and so's your girlfriend
(why do you keep typing
fiend)

their kind
Anne Sexton wrote a poem about them

hurl the book across the room
the cat will shred it
but your girlfriend's got the verse
by heart

you call her
goddess
while you fumble with her bra

she scares you shitless
and in bed
she weaves her spells
she practices her art
transforms you to a mouse
as in a myth

how slowly

some days
how slowly
flows the river
that of consciousness
and i a crumbling cork in it

oh rudderless

i think of all
the swimmers in my streams
some surfers too
all hunted down
white sharks

my screen glows whiter
than potential
clean blank canvas stretched
which i most days
mistake for nothingness

last night
twice
thunder shook the house
an inch of rain
so muggier than hell today.

but after work i saw a fawn
curled cool
in backyard spruce shade

looking at me with intent
or so it seemed

but i admit i often think
that you
are looking at me that way too

you like to say
you're not

imagined pathways

our journeys much like books
we know we need to read
imagined pathways
smooth
or jumbled as a ruin

memories of weeks in Greece

Olympia Mycenae Delphi
the Acropolis and Epidaurus

three blue seas
white sun and stones
gray olive groves

and zooming in
to Alfa beer and belly dancers
Socrates on t shirts
stray dogs roaming Athens

finding sandals
at the poet sandalmaker's
chatting with two Aussies there

the poet's son (a poet too) was in
and fitted me
we traded books

been sixteen years
time floating on the waves
of images and words

leaf light

we walk in greengold leaf light
wife and dog and i

in cool breeze
smaller branches creak
the sound like infants mewling

dreams of bog men flicker through me
i was born too meek for that
for this is only Midwest mud
the dew will rinse our shoes

i bear no spear or sword or shield
my mouth
no taste for blood
a poop bag gloves my good hand
bless my fear

i flex what's left of biceps
pecs
yes time has had its way

i've learned that feelings come
and go
just do your work
no irony

now i imagine music
and a rhyme aslant
in scudding clouds above
that hum
you're lucky lucky lucky lucky lucky

lightning

the streaks of gray like lightning
in your mother's hair
like Elsa Lanchester
The Bride of Frankenstein

you've stomped around like Karloff
all your life
a magpie of a man
an animated corpse

you think you died again
mid 2010s
imagined price of childlessness

your introspection's garnered little
you've had stitches in your head

you've stood in lightning
Texas Iowa and North Dakota
screaming
it's alive

some friends of yours got drunk one night
burned down a farmer's barn
imagine fire reaching heaven
Zeus in anger
hurling it back down some night
as summer lightning

almost half a century ago
you and your redhaired girlfriend
loved beneath
a massive oak tree
later struck by lightning
lost a limb

these branches bolts and veins
in skies in breasts
in backs of parents' hands
now yours

and something quickens in you
pray for rain

mining

hard rain last night
my socks still wet
from walking Trey this morning

now he's panting on the bed
his muddy paws
about to brush my pillowcase

each Sunday's Mental Health Day
chance of rain is 82%
but what about contentment

Mozart on the playlist
Klemperer my favorite conducting

coffee's strong
day's middle cup i'd say

slight ringing in my ears
it's pulse
so i'm alive

big sigh from Trey
i mind my business
mine the minefield
of my mind

though open
my venetian blinds

still slice my vision
like a loaf

ok
my All is only Part

it's broken
like my art

monstrosity

this morning's dogwalk's done
the coffee's gone

your wife is up and down
the basement stairs
just what's she making

dog is zonked of course

Beethoven's in your earphones
overture starts dissonant
gets staid

a Saturday that's misty gray
a bit like you

how will you waste it
dozing with an obtuse book
a twitchy horror film
or will you make
your own monstrosity

you think you've learned
to earn your ironies
as well as your abstractions

lamp reveals more age spots
on your hands

the sun could fry you
like a Hammer vampire

gangrene
evergreen
you still believe you're real
the person writing this

morsels

my boots are waterproof
but this is mud
above the ankle cuff

it's Trey and Ann and i
the morning dogwalk

sunny forty some degrees
the reeds around us grass above us
hibernation beige
but trending tender green

Ann says she smells a skunk
but allergies have stuffed me up

i've chopped my known world
into morsels i can chew

but Trey is stronger willed
he looks a little like Anubis
sniffs beyond the mere quotidian

he ate a baby rabbit yesterday
that's someone's Easter bunny
Ann's dark joke

i'm thinking of our guilty brunch
the pig that died
for my fried ham

nocturne (vi)

the cage i welded fast
so i could rattle it
to hell and back

i'm in it now with Trey
who's black as Cerberus
and snuffling with a knowledge
language cannot hold

thus my confusion
circling back along these paths
with quaking leaves and breaching roots
all manner of the dead
yeast rising underfoot

the night hangs gray as smoke
house lights a mile or more away

small snowflakes and my steaming breath
commingle
in my headlamp's beam

this is the third straight night
i've thought i wouldn't mind
a peaceful death
deep in these woods
or in the stubbly meadow west of here

i've lived too safe
so it won't happen
yet

nocturne (viii)

unscrew your skull
to let red dwarfs
or dumb gods' songs fall in

my darker angel tells me this
the whispers dying to a hum
beyond my outer worlds
and inner hells

i walk the dog
who's black as Cerberus
and in this cold i glow like snow
my breaths condensed to ghosts
that drift to silent deaths
consumed by forces that will murder us

my testicles are snugged up tight
i know you want to know

our twilit insights

think about how all things end
in sadness
how we hope we're wrong

we tiptoe on the brink of madness
thin black ice

we slip sometimes
but love's like this
yes
even when it rhymes

oracles

1

the sky today
an oracle
that you cannot decode

you're looking at its pictures
sipping coffee
one self medication
this Beethoven string quartet
another

the dog is whining on the bed
your child

the tv forecast says high winds a storm
oh you'll survive
unless you don't

you check the football schedule
odds against your favorite team

as if you'd place a bet

you witness and react
you hoard your courage for the odd
creative burst

pale sun
blown grass
a lone bird chirping
engines whirring down the interstate
this data you record

but what's its beauty
use

you ask your gods
if you exist
don't let me waste my life

2

the leaves are turning
planet too
the universe expanding
you however shrivel

leaves are burning
Mahler does this to you
Leonard Cohen
Poe
moribund
with jokes thrown in

now goblet shards
the coffee's cold
you drink the darkness up

your brighter angel
comes to you
all sooty scabbed
your mythic self on Sunday mornings
says
blind seer we know
you think you're lightly here
just passing through
we'd like you to
interrogate your ambiguity
examine your detachment

who does that

you cue up Bruckner on the playlist
hone an axe to split your skull

sublime

the brass the song of gods
if such a thing exists

Prince Edward Island

a walk in north Atlantic shallows
fine red sand of Brackley Beach
we met a lobsterman
Acadian named Claude

a long hike through the Haunted Wood
to Anne's Green Gables house

saw cormorants and cliffs at Orby Head

a short talk with a globetrotting
New Zealand nurse

wolfed down a one pound lobster
saw the pots
then drank good stout at Gahan House

another tourist
said he's kept a travel journal
years and years
i caught him jotting things i said

yes there's a lesson here
we can't absorb all that we sense

still shaking sand from shoes
that i wore new
back then

routine's myths

your wife's on Zoom
the dog is zonked
a beer sweats heavily in front of you

the pot that you call Thumper
rocks with boiling hot linguini
writhing snakes in water

here is where
the everyday transmogrifies

yes that's Medusa on the stovetop
don't dare meet her eyes
your liquid courage won't suffice
so find a mirror
then she dies

outside
a centaur paws the mulch
the pines behind the deck lend shade
to meddling Fates
a Valkyrie rides high above the plates
you left out on the picnic table

lines like these
the Muse has coaxed from you
an art that's cobbled
from the dogged beating heart

tonight's the night

a summer night
the 8 track tape Neil Young
warm beer
you're riding with a friend
from high school days
blue '68 Camaro three on the tree
oh fumbling with the roach clip
highway gone and getting close to town

arrive
a friend of a friend
of a friend of a friend's apartment
it's Commander Cody on the stereo
hashish and whiskey strangers

stumble out
and where's your friend
you meet three women in the driveway
(one of them will be your wife
but that is three years hence)
your vertigo attack
seaswells the earth beneath your feet
to Ahab's deck

next party
only bowls of pills
you check a bedroom
people writhing on the carpet

swipe two pizzas from the freezer
moonlit alley
wake next morning
wearing someone else's jeans

waiting for the sun

a late Beethoven string quartet
with morning coffee

dog is zonked and lying in my bed
oh it's ok
he's like my child

we had a long wet walk
the season's stubborn
overcast and cool

the years have tried
to teach me to be patient

i am living proof
that wisdom
doesn't always with come
with age

most nights i see my breath
it's blacker than light's absence
aberration's blaze
to tell me that my shadow
still lives strong within me
molding all my necessary masks

no shame
the sane self medicate
and cope

and look
sky's brightening

believe it
all of us are suffering
the same

wants

been thinking once again
about my parents

Dad's old pasta pot
the one that i've named Thumper
does its thing

a bag of penne
squats like Buddha
on the kitchen counter

Mahler's on the playlist
all that beauty overripe

i slice tomatoes
a good friend has given me
like weeping planets in my hands

the knife's Dad's too
no it's not
i want it to be

*

so Dad liked Mom in red

she had a dress she rarely wore
preferred dark blue

good dancer
Elvis fan
she smoked two packs a day
for decades

kisses smelled like death
i didn't mind

her mother cooked for parish priests

her sister's father
was not her mother's husband
so a family rumor went

you want more clarity
so do i

workshop

the setting sun bleeds gold
between the pines
that darken in the breeze

and i am not
the person
that i was
when i began this thought

here sitting with me
Sandy
not the same
but someone new

and Sally Mona William
and Diane
are you still you
right no

and yes

all vying for a space
in my small closet
of a brain

though not born sad
i do believe
that all things end
in sadness

am i wrong

i suck my gut in
lift my chins
heave out my chest

but i am melting
like a movie witch
and everything's all smashed together
morphing as it mashes

this rough draft
of a life
a poet's hash

you're not even here

it's why i write about you now

near zeroes of your deathbeds
one of you so swollen wracked
you couldn't even look at me
the other swirled in tides of incoherence
we were talking underwater

friends and i read other people's poems
beat them with a rubber hose
to see how art creates safe spaces
where we all can say and feel the things
that might just kill us in the everyday
grief guilt and shame

for me it's not the missed i love yous
maybe not

not even missing you

it's just that i've felt freer

with you gone

II.

from a nightmare notebook

among the fallen maple leaves
a withered hand

*

beheaded king
the crown
still rattling

*

blood moon
and two red eyes
in sighing pines

*

dead lover's scent
a spider
on the pillow's cooler side

*

fat worm
where
your tongue once was

*

hard rain tonight
all the dead poets
typing

*

in the mirror
only darkness
where your face should be

*

string quartet
sawing pine boards
for your coffin

*

wet dream
your swollen corpse breaks through
the river ice

*

your ouija board tattoos
i kiss my dead
to life

Dada moves

after

ripples
pebble water
in orbit the next

*

blame

says i
myself in weakness
sense assert
alone

*

catafalque

frayed book whispers
tune every bedside sky black

*

elect tic

a
count

a
mount

n
crypt
id

*

grammacide

smothersmothers' mothers

*

not a leap year

clouds coffee
        fall fly

like love
        rain
specked stalling
        tired

too to
        your window

*

p r tr t

n th m r r
( )
wh r y r f c sh d b

*

réponse

sky's
rounded shoulders
shrug

*

setting broken dispatch

clouds sitting with you
you should talk
there's not a money side

*

swordswords

*

whirred wore

roe bought / maid high coo / sawn nets / past aweigh / know
testy calls

*

year's end

mount the last mixed guilt
the scrubbed muse the worried shade
pass memory here

III.

across the Mississippi

brown skeletons awaiting better days
the way you see the trees

friends stoking you
with coffee in the morning
beer at night

good morrow and good morrow
and good morrow
chugging like full tugboats

cellphone photos of the Mississippi River
snapped quick from the car

they slide across your mind
chunked blue ice
blurred
by motion
sun
like aging eyes
or stars on windy nights

infinity still undiminished
loss gapes wide
then morphs into discovery

just face the whole
be done with crossing out

great sex this morning
Catholic wake this evening

family from the south and west descend
this house sleeps ten

after all

you're reading Aeschylus
the coffee almost gone
you think the gods are just your needs
yes forces large enough
to topple royal houses

wife reminds you that on Monday
workmen come again to mend
the siding
deck and porch
and *Hamlet* essays still to grade

just say the sky has fallen
like a shingle
maybe you've contracted shingles
fine

your pain and hunger ripple out
the Chorus fans the Furies

flames and sulfur eat your tongues
and yes you've killed your young

that is
the younger versions
of yourselves

you want to kiss her now
it's lovely here in fall
you're not so tragic after all

beneath Orion

the dog and you trot hard
through muddy woods

to think in threes is best
say wiser minds than yours
and you are dark with matter
waves and particles
of what you've read and lived

cross country runners
panting here
when weather's fair

gray clumps of feathers
deer cull ghosts
a sky that bleeds
warm CO_2
pale blue
between scrub pines

all flow so small
beneath Orion
in the southward nighttime sky
this time of year

superposition bends you
there
and there
and yet you're here

you're one of three
with dog and wife
still hunting for a measure
true enough to trust
starlight you see
wish fresh
yet aged a hundred years

black coffee and Bob Dylan

living hard
within your element's
not easy

bend your mind
you must

the beer and poetry come later

sex a vision
bed an open boat on open sea
the steady furrows
glisten
pitch
the fins and teeth below
an island or a continent
offstage

your little tragicomedy
you almost die
get married
fall in love
are stalked by sharks
not sure about the order
more a loop perhaps

you thrash and flop
get bitten
exit neither left nor right

the folk song hits the bridge
it's burning

magic's everywhere
but darkens quickly
into night

blurred picture

tonight you're just too jumpy for a selfie

take a picture of your wife instead
she's grimacing
no
surely that's a smile

your third beer in
and Glenn Gould's Bach is rippling
from the playlist

what did Mother do
with your umbilical
the wedding ring you've lately polished
smells a lot like blood

your neutered greyhound
won't stop licking at his crotch
it could be allergies
your meds have quelled your own

cheer up
there's whiskey
in the kitchen cabinet
below the dripping sink

night sky is rubbed with Vaseline
your wife is warming
to the talk of next year's big remodel
find her lips and kiss

break the music

amygdalae and synapses
you break the music of the spheres
with rack and thumbscrew idiolect

sounds fresh
better than tennis without a net

your wife reminds you though
the sun
the nothing new
that's ever under it

she's right

the Eiffel Tower
Bay of Fundy
Scottish Highlands
Parthenon
the Western world
you've seen in bits and bobs

you try to haul it in
to shore these fragments up
against your ruins

it's heroic
and absurd

some music makes you want to cry
you won't
but that's another poem

right now
it's Brian Eno on the playlist
reshaping ambiences
you should share

broken record

but that ol' way don't work no mo'
an earworm blues insists
the spell like one of John Lee Hooker's
cooking slowly
spices biting psyche
inciting flesh

you wish you were with her

instead
a horseshoe booth
brewpub snuggery
midtown Detroit
with Zach and Tyler
three headed monster
talking music poetry and social justice
god help you

change will come
like backyard birdsong
northern woods' bootsucking mud
the wandering planets in the blood

the server brings you Belgian ale
your third

you text her pictures
of the record pressing plant you've visited
it's retro chic
producing art that spins like wheels

buffalo

these days you feel the need
to stare an animal in the eyes
be eaten even
wear its pelt or fill its belly

no
it's not the whiskey talking
cabin fever maybe

that buffalo was bigger than our Subaru
you say
your wife and you remembering
your North Dakota days

they're bison honey look it up
you do
she's right

but so's your urge for juices
something
flowing
doing

evil is banal
and virtue is a luxury
but binaries are not enough

the landscape
mindscape

scapegoat
great escape
all stark
but fossil rich
big skyed

you wondered how you'd finish life
not wise
amazed

California ghosts

that Escondido open mic
wife's nephew killed it on guitar
you kept your folded poems
pale vagina
in your pocket
sunburned forehead flaking snow

you're drinking local beers
you brought back warm
and packed like ingots in your dirty clothes

when flying in and out
you saw the ocean
never touched it

socks got wet while walking shoeless
drunk
in midnight rain
around that gated subdivision

cellphone photos just a husk
the wispy ghosts appear
between the ears
the hauntings of all travelers
so lightly here

last morning hike
your brother's wife said
god your legs are so damned white

clockface

the bedroom ceiling fan
the clockface of your lives

the time
glints whirrs and clicks
like blades above your heads

it's like a tale by Poe
the dead things won't stay dead

the way you hear
the playlist string quartet
abuzz with saws
viola violins and cello
making coffins

dying planet
lying politicians
eat your brainspace
that's the wake you keep

wheels turn
the basement flooded
power gone out

on cool and starry nights
your household demons
mock you with their slumber
docked tight in your skulls

when fully charged
they hit Repeat
and snow will bury reason
drought will torch belief

you skip that blissful season
sleep

conjurings

this string quartet
spiked collar
coffee cup
a muzzle

wife's out with the dog
the season's cold

forgot what warms you up

don't let the poem mope
you tell yourself
and be a smith of myths
the wick is lit
the wit's not licked

a witch or goddess
succubus or muse
you conjure them
but dream they'll come unbidden

here at this home office window
you could be a maiden in a castle tower
a painter at a breathing easel
blue and green the view
the sky on top of trees
that shudder making love

old sadness and new life
the fall and spring
so beautiful
if you don't mind the mud

crooked highways

tonight beers two thirds gone
just like your lives
you contemplate senility

my groove's become a rut
you say
a line you wrote so many years ago

relax
she says
there's Dylan on the stereo

relax
it's always Now
your mantras
comforting but trite

the wind's just right
you hear the tires whining on the interstate

Bob too
i've walked and i've crawled
on six crooked highways

traveling you've loved to play this game
you see a weird car
or weird people in a roadside bar
and one of you will ask the other
wonder where they're going

how many times
you've asked it of yourselves

deep Montana

you've stepped into a pool of silence
deep Montana

haze from distant fires

high up there
above the treeline
speck of white
a mountain goat
a patch of snow
won't know unless it moves

you've eaten huckleberries
thimbleberries
heard you could survive
on old man's beard in dire times

you've seen a black bear flipping stones
along the shore of Waterton
bald eagle
osprey

bighorn rams have butted heads
before your eyes at Logan Pass
the sound a muted gunshot

later
ewes and kids

fifteen or twenty
trotted past you at Two Medicine

as if you needed proof
that you were healed

evangelical home

a misty night
a little wind
and too much black and slick
tough driving town to town
without a buzz

you bring a toothbrush and
a peanut butter sandwich
cell phone charger
murder novel

dog's in back
you've cracked the windows
he can poke his nose and sniff
the mystery of dark and wet

a roundabout
a lightless stretch
a flashing yellow
truck lights in the rearview mirror
scherzo on the playlist
whoosh of cranked defrost

to feel a rhythm to your consciousness
to beat or meet your short deadlines
no answers
only comfort

then
so soon
arrival

you kiss your wife
at her mother's deathbed

exterminator

exterminator came this afternoon
his poison killed the yellow jackets nesting
in your northern soffit

now you're on your second beer
late Dylan playing soft

you're thinking
terminus
the yield from years of teaching
Oedipus
Macbeth and *Lear*
dark ambiguity

your wife is looking for
what feeds her soul
you get it
but you're gorged on tragic weird
yours

mud daubers plagued your other house
years younger then
you sprayed them all
ran manic down the driveway
while they died

most love's dried mud
cicadas thriving underground
the rising terrifying
till you all adjust
to so much light and sound

fate

a friend's friend's tarot deck
your childhood Ouija board
the entrails the diviner probes
benighted omens
prompted by the beer
in front of you
they call it red
it looks like rust

it's garbage night
Neil Young is on the stereo
Old Man

your wife is gone
a wine and watercolor workshop
with some girlfriends

dog is stuck with you
his muzzle gray as yours
and both of you with bum left knees

you sip
it seems that someone flicked
a switch and made you old

you've told your buddy Zach
you don't mind dying any time
you're satisfied

reminds you of a blues
a college friend
a guy named Fate
would play

leave a record

sure
entropy increases
all devolves to chaos
so the science says

but just imagine
meshed and shining gears of heaven
mind a perfect clock

your greyhound
rapt
is chomping on a bone

your wife's tap tapping
at a tablet

you're upstairs
and someone on the playlist's sawing
at a Shostakovich string quartet

you thrash inside these bodies
chance has stuffed you in

these bodies
that appall so often
that so often
guide you to the lightning strike of joy

so

singed or soiled
you know you are alive

such pleasant pain you take
to leave a record
even one a mouse click can erase

the moon's no help

the dark outside
has made the windows mirrors

slight chill curls around your legs
a shark that visits when you fret

the hope that keeps you bundled tight
is knotted twice but fraying

all your friends self medicate

you do the same
strong coffee in the morning
stronger beer and sometimes scotch at night

your wife has got a shoe that squeaks
you hear it now

and now the clicking
of a leash's metal lobster claw

you walk
the moon's no help
it only makes the dog go loco

now where
drifts
to nowhere

whine of tires
on the nearby interstate
crescendos
ebbs
then rolls and darkens
like the ocean's moan

no confessional

car keys on the bar
a Citizen on your wrist
a Visa in your pocket
fine

be something
besides a beast
you think you hear your culture say

but big screen football's blaring louder

everybody's talking
words that undergird or sugarcoat

this barrel aged stout
is bringing something out
you feel ambivalent about
like listening to Tchaikovsky

how to work this off
like debt

there's no confessional
you hit the pretzels hard
maintain a half assed Buddhist calm

you still want burning
want to kiss her ear at least

when she comes back
a call she said she had to take

her hair a shock of wheat
that smells of rye

you're married

but to other people

no judgment

you thank the gods
or fate
for letting you live
this

you love it mostly
not sure what it means

a blackness fills the evergreens out back
and scabs of snow glow soft as moons
reflecting last year's Christmas lights

yes night is falling
and you feel a sweetness
with a double shot of sadness in it
been like this all day
all life

your wife is gone
the dog's been walked
a slight hangover

almost overwhelming trying to assert yourself
in such a universe
not tragic
only small heroics

third beer biting back
you hear John Fahey on the playlist
Blind Joe Death transfigured

night moves
with no judgment yet

a poem or something

the blackbirds and the mourning doves
that haunt the backyard feeder
have you thinking
need
the burning fuse that drives us all

and even though right now
it's wan and shackled in the pines
the sun's a brooding Samson

Music for 18 Musicians
bleeps and burbles from the speakers
percolating coffee
for your spirit

jingling tags
the dog has roused himself from sleep
your wife will take him out
he's still a puppy
new love of her life

you barbecued in gentle rain last night
good friends of many years were over
drinking talking late

you'd love to make a poem
or something of yourself
today

renewing the vows

so John Lee Hooker's singing
bourbon
scotch and beer
he wants to get drunk
get her off his mind

you're sipping water
neat

when she comes back
it's just as Emily says
wild nights and luxury

a dog yelp down the block
and bird squawks in the dimming trees
the day's been mist
and dark's an hour off

could call it haunted
office loft a moldered turret
you a patriarch of poltergeists

more likely you're the luckless guest
fat hands and nervous sweat

a groom splayed facedown on the altar
monk gone barking mad

you need her now
the attic's sour pall her veil
to set the place ablaze
to say
i do

revised forecast

long misty day ahead
new age spots on your veiny hand backs
baggy eyes
the smile lines
harbingers of jowls

just maybe
when the storm kicks up
you'll do your Lear
get naked
howl along
a bare forked animal
in need

but now
you hear a plate clank in the kitchen
scrape of knife on toast

downstairs
your wife flips through a catalog
your mind's eye sees her
lick her middle finger

a friar
local news this morning says
will be beatified today

a plane or thunder
rumbles overhead

the backyard spruce trees sway
so dark
so deep
the way they keep their green
a minor miracle

small beads
of rain
now tremble all along the eaves

shelter

Baudelaire lies steaming
on the bedside table

Dylan sang hard rain on you
from Davenport to Battle Creek

a storm a guest
without departure date
and shelter just a curtain
caught between the claps

you taste the solubility
of skin in air
of words in silence

neighbors' houses melting slowly
down the blocks
like butter lambs in frying pans

chorizo and manchego
on the cutting board
green grapes
cheap burgundy
the harder stuff
you'll want to hit so soon
all cool as pillows
in long marriages

you've fizzed like salmon in the river
hugged the driftwood in the flood

been lost
thought drowned

grown legs
been found

some nights you float

your skeletons like ice
like hollow alabaster statues

bobbing shallowly
inside your hairy bags
of blood and skin
hopes leaking out the pores
and soaking sheets

the dream of gills
red fangs or claws
still clings like scent

the mind wilds
heaven of the darkest
musky angels
ribbed with cunning
evanescent as the tinctures
that you vape

but now your bodies rocking
coffin in the swollen waters
iron cage
that you and need
have welded stoutly
never thinking of a door

those antlered
trophies mounted on the chamber wall
one gaze at you
they yawn and look away

the space between you

it isn't far from ear to ear
yet everything that you can see
Loch Ness
Grand Tetons
or Manhattan skyline
fits inside your head

Orion strides above the arborvitae
saw it with the dog out back

and now
you're sitting on the couch
a second beer half gone

your wife intently doing something
on her phone

the space between you
feet or universes
likely worlds curved weirdly
and overlapping
ghosts commingling in the drift

as Hamlet says
let be

the secret to a happy marriage
keep your mouth shut

wisdom of the elders
ancient eyes your stars
or did you see this on tv

this blue ballpoint

it glides just like your tongue
between her breasts in better days
on wilder nights

and oh to moor in thee
as Emily exclaims

but such allusions dog you
while you're listening to Archie Shepp
his Coltrane homage not as edgy
as you bet it was
in '64

that year you lived in Turkey
army brat
whose mom was hot enough
to get her ass pinched
by the locals in the market

later
Dad in Vietnam
the '60s spooling out like torn intestines

crack a few less beers
and love the world a little more
you want to tell those two
those three
those four

they're dead
it's why you write

to live again

strange days and stranger nights
you wouldn't mind it weirder
a whiskey in your hand
and her
well
out of hand
at least you wish it so

a jazzman's on the stereo
he's murdering the standards
with piano
bass and drums
complicit in the act

it's Night and Day
and Tea for Two
I've Got You under My Skin

you think the world will kill you quick
but really it just eats you slow
just like you sip

there's chicken in the fridge
you'll chop some greens

relax
if you sleep hard enough

it's like you're dead
except you get to live again

you rise a little faded
but a kiss will bring the color back

under house arrest

the dog still sick
your wife gone
to Chicago
will she even come back home

the breeze high in the trees
you hear it sighing
throws the sunshine straight down through
the skylight
dappled waves

i'm under god's own microscope
you'd say if you believed

but this and you are something grainier
daguerreotype
kinetoscope
dark matter everywhere to contemplate

you texted
back and forth last night
buck up
she wrote she loved you

don't you know

it's why you're playing Mahler
channeling Prince Hamlet now
hope's music overripe
space time's collapse
a consummation devoutly to be wished

under reconstruction

alone you sip strong beer
arrange the under reconstruction
life with her
you tore apart so long ago
that you've forgotten
how it fits together

piles of glinting parts
as beautiful as weaponry
to pacifists

outside the kitchen window
siding slats
old baby boomer beige
new cream of the millennials

the house has shed its skin

last night
hair stylist buzzed you good
the clippers set at
four
unlucky number
close to Chinese word for
death

now
something fanged and coiled in you

whispers
serendipitous

you see
among the sloughed off
selves
a bright new love
hissing

www.ingramcontent.com/pod-product-compliance
Lightning Source LLC
LaVergne TN
LVHW051442170726
843492LV00002B/509